" Contents "

« Introduction »

LEAFING THROUGH THE WISE AND WITTY WORDS IN THIS BOOK, you could be forgiven for starting to think that some people talk only in small, utterly quotable, bite-sized chunks. Did Groucho Marx or Oscar Wilde ever say anything that wasn't pithy, funny and less than twenty-five words? It would have made a conversation with either of them at first hilarious, then completely exhausting, then thoroughly irritating. Perhaps, for some people, that is exactly how they came across. Had they ever met (they never did, Groucho Marx was a ten-year-old growing up in New York when Oscar Wilde died in Paris in 1900) it is tempting to imagine a duel of quips erupting with the zing of rapier wit slashing through the air. On the other hand, they might have had little to say to each other, choosing to save their sharpest lines for a time when they could be used to best advantage, rather than being lost to an opponent's timely response.

Save their best lines? Surely the off-the-cuff, impromptu remarks of the wise and witty personalities featured in this book couldn't possibly have been preconceived? Surely these words couldn't have been processed, prepared and pre-seasoned like a microwave meal-for-one? A skilfully delivered witticism will sound exactly like the orator has plucked it out of the air, but don't be fooled – that really isn't always the case. A comedian on television, or on radio, knows that he can crack a joke or use a witty one-liner only once if he wants it to sound spontaneous. If he uses that remark again on another TV show or when he is appearing live, he can count on a large number of people in the audience starting to mutter about having heard him

WISE & WITTY WORDS

ON LOVE, FAMILY, FRIENDS

WISE & WITTY WORDS

ON LOVE, FAMILY, FRIENDS

OVER 500 QUOTES FROM THE CLEVER, FUNNY
AND FAMOUS, FROM HOMER TO OBAMA

PUBLISHED BY

The Reader's Digest Association, Inc.

LONDON • NEW YORK • SYDNEY • MONTREAL

Wise & Witty Words
Published in 2011 in the United Kingdom by Vivat Direct Limited
(t/a Reader's Digest), 157 Edgware Road, London W2 2HR

Wise & Witty Words is based on material taken from *The Big Book of Wit and Wisdom*
published by The Reader's Digest Association Limited in 2009.

We are committed both to the quality of our products and the service we provide
to our customers. We value your comments, so please do contact us
on 0871 351 1000 or via our website at www.readersdigest.co.uk
If you have any comments or suggestions about the content of our books,
email us at gbeditorial@readersdigest.co.uk

FOR VIVAT DIRECT
PROJECT EDITORS: Rod Green and Penny Craig
DESIGNER: Sailesh Patel
PROOFREADER: Barry Gage
EDITORIAL DIRECTOR: Julian Browne
ART DIRECTOR: Anne-Marie Bulat
MANAGING EDITOR: Nina Hathway
PREPRESS TECHNICAL MANAGER: Dean Russell
PRODUCTION CONTROLLER: Jan Bucil

COVER ILLUSTRATION AND TYPOGRAPHY: Victoria Sawdon

Printing and binding Arvato Iberia, Portugal

ISBN: 978 1 78020 042 2
BOOK CODE: 400-550-UP0000 1

deliver that line before. Sometimes, if the quip has been worked into a routine, he'll do it anyway. Audiences often enjoy familiar material because it helps them to know when they can laugh. Nobody wants to be the only one laughing at the wrong time during a performance. A little familiarity with the comedian's material can be a good thing.

Don't think, however, that the gag was completely fresh first time round. Comedians who appear on panel shows on TV or radio have a stock of gags in their heads that they can raid whenever the occasion arises. Their artistry is in writing the material in the first place and the practised skill is in choosing the right moment to use it. Some gags might simply go past their 'sell by date' without ever seeing the light of day. In other cases, the performer might gently manipulate the conversation until he can slip his gag in, looking like it has just come off the top of his head. Spontaneity needs to be carefully planned.

That doesn't mean to say, of course, that the most talented wits are not able to react to what others are saying with lively, fresh, quotable quips. They undoubtedly do, and will be quoted extensively, although not necessarily accurately, the following evening in pubs all over the country.

Comedians are not the only people quoted in this book. They are not the only people to deliver funny lines and, indeed, wise as well as funny lines are quoted within these pages. The words of wisdom come from famous people in all walks of life but, as you might expect, politicians, statesmen and philosophers are well represented. In a way, many of those quoted, use the same technique as the comedian, preparing their spontaneous statements well in advance. Nowadays these often come across in what are known as 'sound bites'. A sound bite is a short phrase that captures the essence of what the speaker has to say. Deliberately designed for maximum impact from as few words as possible, a good sound bite not only captures that essence, but also captures headlines and, in turn, captures as much publicity for the speaker as it is possible to squeeze out of one short speech.

British Prime Minister Tony Blair, commenting on the importance of the Good Friday agreement to the peace process in Northern Ireland, stated in his speech that, 'A day like today is not a day for sound bites,' then followed up that statement with, 'I feel the hand of history upon our shoulders.'

A cynical attempt to grab the headlines? Surely no politician would pull a stunt like that . . .would he?

Another thing that comedians, politicians, celebrities, academics and philosophers from every walk of life do is to quote each other. It lends a certain authority to what you are saying if you can throw in a quote or two from someone whom everyone trusts to know what he is talking about. That way you can borrow a bit of trust to help win over your audience.

Whether you are dipping into this book purely for entertainment, or whether you are looking for a few quotes to slip into a speech at a family function, there is a wealth of material from an army of familiar names to browse through – some profound, some thought-provoking, some just downright silly. Enjoy them all and perhaps the wise and witty words of others will inspire you to create some quotable gems of your own!

" LOVE "

'Tis better to have loved and lost than never to have loved at all.

ALFRED,
LORD TENNYSON

"It's Only Love"

Love is an irresistible desire
to be irresistibly desired.
ROBERT FROST

*No, there's nothing
half so sweet in life
As love's young dream.*
THOMAS MOORE

Love is the triumph
of imagination over intelligence.
H.L. MENCKEN

"It's Only Love"

**MY WIFE AND I THOUGHT THAT
WE WERE IN LOVE BUT IT TURNED OUT
TO BE BENIGN.**

WOODY ALLEN

Men seldom make passes
at girls who wear glasses.

DOROTHY PARKER

A kiss is a lovely trick designed
by nature to stop speech when
words become superfluous.

INGRID BERGMAN

**TO FALL IN LOVE IS TO CREATE
A RELIGION THAT HAS A FALLIBLE GOD.**

JORGE LUIS BORGES

"LOVE"

One is very crazy when in love.

SIGMUND FREUD

Once in his life, every man is entitled to
fall madly in love with a gorgeous redhead.

LUCILLE BALL

A pair of powerful spectacles
has sometimes sufficed
to cure a person in love.

FRIEDRICH NIETZSCHE

*Love conquers all things . . .
except poverty and toothache.*

MAE WEST

"It's Only Love"

LOVE IS UNIVERSAL MIGRAINE, A BRIGHT STAIN ON THE VISION BLOTTING OUT REASON.

ROBERT GRAVES

Only one kind of love lasts . . . unrequited.

SOMERSET MAUGHAM

Love is a fire. But whether it is going to warm your hearth or burn down your house, you can never tell.

JOAN CRAWFORD

ALL LOVE SHIFTS AND CHANGES.
I DON'T KNOW IF YOU CAN BE
WHOLEHEARTEDLY IN LOVE ALL THE TIME.

JULIE ANDREWS

"LOVE"

A guy knows he's in love when he loses interest in his car for a couple of days.

TIM ALLEN

When you love a man, he becomes more than a body.
His physical limbs expand, and his outline recedes, vanishes.
He is rich and sweet and right. He is part of the world,
the atmosphere, the blue sky and the blue water.

GWENDOLYN BROOKS

I was born when you kissed me.
I died when you left me. I lived a
few weeks while you loved me.

HUMPHREY BOGART

The best thing to hold onto
in life is each other.

AUDREY HEPBURN

"It's Only Love"

**THERE IS A PLACE YOU CAN TOUCH A WOMAN
THAT WILL DRIVE HER CRAZY. HER HEART.**

MELANIE GRIFFITH

The sound of a kiss is not so loud as that of a
cannon, but its echo lasts a great deal longer.

OLIVER WENDELL HOLMES

The fickleness of the women
I love is only equalled by
the infernal constancy of the
women who love me.

GEORGE BERNARD SHAW

IN LOVE, ONE AND ONE ARE ONE.

JEAN-PAUL SARTRE

"LOVE"

**A man is already halfway in love
with any woman who listens to him.**
BRENDAN FRANCIS

I HERE AND NOW, FINALLY AND FOREVER,
GIVE UP KNOWING ANYTHING ABOUT
LOVE, OR WANTING TO KNOW.
I BELIEVE IT DOESN'T EXIST, SAVE AS A WORD.
IT'S A SORT OF WAILING PHOENIX THAT IS
REALLY THE WIND IN THE TREES.
D.H. LAWRENCE

I don't want to live.
I want to love first,
and live incidentally.
ZELDA FITZGERALD

I would worship the ground
that you walked on, if only you
lived in a better neighbourhood.
BILLY WILDER

"It's Only Love"

YOU WILL FIND AS YOU LOOK BACK UPON YOUR LIFE
THAT THE MOMENTS WHEN YOU HAVE TRULY LIVED
ARE THE MOMENTS WHEN YOU HAVE DONE THINGS
IN THE SPIRIT OF LOVE.

HENRY DRUMMOND

Love is an exploding cigar we willingly smoke.

LYNDA BARRY

The first duty of love is to listen.

PAUL TILLICH

LOVE IS A TEMPORARY INSANITY CURABLE BY MARRIAGE.

AMBROSE BIERCE

"LOVE"

**Looking back, I have this to regret,
that too often when I loved, I did not say so.**
DAVID GRAYSON

Love him and let him love you.
Do you think anything else
under heaven really matters?
JAMES BALDWIN

YOU NEVER LOSE BY LOVING.
YOU ALWAYS LOSE BY HOLDING BACK.
BARBARA DE ANGELIS

If love is the answer,
could you please rephrase
the question?
LILY TOMLIN

"It's Only Love"

I WONDER WHAT FOOL IT WAS THAT FIRST INVENTED KISSING.
JONATHAN SWIFT

Never pretend to a love which you do not actually feel, for love is not ours to command.
ALAN WATTS

Love is an act of endless forgiveness, a tender look which becomes a habit.
PETER USTINOV

LOVE IS A PERKY ELF DANCING A MERRY LITTLE JIG AND THEN SUDDENLY HE TURNS ON YOU WITH A MINIATURE MACHINE GUN.
MATT GROENING

this is page
19

"LOVE"

Love doesn't just sit there, like a stone; it has to be made, like bread, remade all the time, made new.

URSULA K. LE GUIN

Among those whom I like or admire, I can find no common denominator, but among those whom I love, I can: all of them make me laugh.

W.H.AUDEN

There is love, of course.
And then there's life, its enemy.

JEAN ANOUILH

People are unreasonable, illogical, and self-centred. Love them anyway.

MOTHER TERESA

"It's Only Love"

**Love is staying up all night
with a sick child
– or a healthy adult.**

DAVID FROST

LOVE BUILDS BRIDGES WHERE THERE ARE NONE.

R.H. DELANEY

I have a very strong feeling
that the opposite of love
is not hate – it's apathy.
It's not giving a damn.

LEO BUSCAGLIA

The heart of another is a dark forest, always,
no matter how close it has been to one's own.

WILLA CATHER

"LOVE"

It is not love that is blind, but jealousy.
LAWRENCE DURRELL

Love is patient, love is kind. It does not envy, it does not
boast, it is not proud. It is not rude, it is not self-seeking,
it is not easily angered, it keeps no record of wrongs.
Love does not delight in evil but rejoices with the truth.
It always protects, always trusts, always hopes,
always perseveres. Love never fails.

THE BIBLE (I CORINTHIANS)

Passion is the quickest to develop,
and the quickest to fade.
Intimacy develops more slowly,
and commitment more gradually still.

ROBERT STERNBERG

*Nothing spoils a romance so much
as a sense of humour in the woman
– or the want of it in the man.*

OSCAR WILDE

you're on page
22

"It's Only Love"

**IN REAL LOVE YOU WANT
THE OTHER PERSON'S GOOD.
IN ROMANTIC LOVE YOU WANT
THE OTHER PERSON.**
MARGARET ANDERSON

Love is a fan club with only two fans.
ADRIAN HENRI

Always carry a book on a date
so that when you get bored
you can slip into the
Ladies for a read.
SHARON STONE

**IF GRASS CAN GROW THROUGH CEMENT, LOVE CAN
FIND YOU AT EVERY TIME IN YOUR LIFE.**
CHER

"LOVE"

*To love oneself is the beginning
of a lifelong romance.*

OSCAR WILDE

One word frees us of all
the weight and pain of life
– that word is love.

SOPHOCLES

A career is wonderful,
but you can't curl up
with it on a cold night.

MARILYN MONROE

We must love one another or die.

W.H. AUDEN

"It's Only Love"

WHO, BEING LOVED, IS POOR?
OSCAR WILDE

The mark of a true crush
is that you fall in love first
and grope for reasons afterward.
SHANA ALEXANDER

A woman in love can't be reasonable –
or she probably wouldn't be in love.
MAE WEST

MANY YEARS AGO I CHASED A WOMAN
FOR ALMOST TWO YEARS, ONLY TO DISCOVER
THAT HER TASTES WERE EXACTLY LIKE MINE:
WE BOTH WERE CRAZY ABOUT GIRLS.
GROUCHO MARX

Love is like a cigar.
If it goes out, you can light it again
– but it never tastes quite the same.

LORD WAVELL

Love is not enough.
It must be the foundation, the cornerstone
– but not the complete structure.
It is much too pliable, too yielding.

QUENTIN CRISP

There is no reciprocity.
Men love women,
women love children,
children love hamsters.

ALICE THOMAS ELLIS

Sigh no more, ladies, sigh no more,
Men were deceivers ever,
One foot in sea and one on shore,
To one thing constant never.

WILLIAM SHAKESPEARE

"What's Love Got To Do With It?"

Sex without love
is an empty experience,
but as empty experiences go
it's a pretty good one.

WOODY ALLEN

*Sex on television
can't hurt you
unless you fall off.*

ANONYMOUS

I USED TO BE SNOW WHITE
... BUT I DRIFTED.

MAE WEST

"LOVE"

Intimate relationships cannot substitute for a life plan. But to have any meaning or viability at all, a life plan must include intimate relationships.

HARRIET LERNER

Pursuit and seduction are
the essence of sexuality.
It's part of the sizzle.

CAMILLE PAGLIA

The only unnatural sex act is
that which you cannot perform.

ALFRED KINSEY

I BELIEVE THAT SEX IS THE MOST
BEAUTIFUL, NATURAL, WHOLESOME
THING THAT MONEY CAN BUY.

STEVE MARTIN

"What's Love Got To Do With It?"

**IF ALL THE GIRLS WHO ATTENDED
THE YALE PROM WERE LAID END TO END,
I WOULDN'T BE AT ALL SURPRISED.**

DOROTHY PARKER

I often think that a slightly exposed shoulder
emerging from a long satin nightgown packs
more sex than two naked bodies in bed.

BETTE DAVIS

My wife and I have Olympic sex
. . . once every four years.

RODNEY DANGERFIELD

WHATEVER ELSE CAN
BE SAID ABOUT SEX,
IT CANNOT BE CALLED
A DIGNIFIED PERFORMANCE.

HELEN LAWRENSON

"LOVE"

Sex alleviates tension.
Love causes it.

WOODY ALLEN

If you want sex, have an affair.
If you want a relationship, buy a dog.

JULIE BURCHILL

A woman making up her lips
is like a soldier preparing
his machine gun.

SIGMUND FREUD

Two's company.
Three's fifty bucks.

JOAN RIVERS

"What's Love Got To Do With It?"

**THERE IS NOTHING LIKE
EARLY PROMISCUOUS SEX FOR DISPELLING
LIFE'S BRIGHT MYSTERIOUS EXPECTATIONS.**

IRIS MURDOCH

ALL HUMAN BEINGS
CONNECT SEX AND LOVE
. . . EXCEPT FOR MEN.

ROSEANNE BARR

Chastity: the most unnatural
of the sexual perversions.

ALDOUS HUXLEY

**I KNOW NOTHING ABOUT SEX
BECAUSE I WAS ALWAYS MARRIED.**

ZSA ZSA GABOR

"LOVE"

In America sex is an obsession,
in other parts of the world it is a fact.

MARLENE DIETRICH

IT'S OKAY TO LAUGH IN THE BEDROOM
AS LONG AS YOU DON'T POINT.

WILL DURST

Among men, sex sometimes
results in intimacy; among women,
intimacy sometimes results in sex.

BARBARA CARTLAND

I married a German.
Every night I dress up
as Poland and he invades me.

BETTE MIDLER

"What's Love Got To Do With It?"

MEN WHO ARE TOO GOOD LOOKING ARE NEVER GOOD IN BED BECAUSE THEY NEVER HAD TO BE.
CINDY CHUPACK

Men lose more conquests by their own awkwardness than by any virtue in the woman.
NINON DE LENCLOS

A woman's most erogenous zone is her mind.
RAQUEL WELCH

I'M ALWAYS LOOKING FOR MEANINGFUL ONE-NIGHT STANDS.
DUDLEY MOORE

Pornography is rather like trying to find out about a Beethoven symphony by having somebody tell you about it and perhaps hum a few bars.
ROBERTSON DAVIES

In my sex fantasy, nobody ever loves me for my mind.
NORA EPHRON

My wife is a sex object. Every time I ask her for sex, she objects.
LES DAWSON

Women need a reason to have sex. Men just need a place.
BILLY CRYSTAL

"What's Love Got To Do With It?"

**SEX: THE THING THAT TAKES UP
THE LEAST AMOUNT OF TIME AND
CAUSES THE MOST AMOUNT OF TROUBLE.**

JOHN BARRYMORE

The thing that women like most
in bed is breakfast.

ROBIN WILLIAMS

Brevity is the soul of lingerie.

DOROTHY PARKER

**I'VE BEEN ON MORE LAPS
THAN A NAPKIN.**

MAE WEST

"LOVE"

Sex is a momentary itch;
love never lets you go.

KINGSLEY AMIS

Sex has never been an obsession with me.
It's just like eating a bag of crisps.
Quite nice, but nothing marvellous.

BOY GEORGE

I only like two kinds of men:
domestic and foreign.

MAE WEST

Love is the answer, but
while you're waiting for the answer,
sex raises some pretty interesting questions.

WOODY ALLEN

"What's Love Got To Do With It?"

ONE MORE DRINK AND I'D HAVE BEEN UNDER THE HOST.
DOROTHY PARKER

There is, of course, no reason for the existence of the male sex except that sometimes one needs help with moving the piano.
REBECCA WEST

I'm a lesbian trapped in a man's body.
EDDIE IZZARD

WHETHER HE ADMITS IT OR NOT,
A MAN HAS BEEN BROUGHT UP TO LOOK
AT MONEY AS A SIGN OF HIS VIRILITY,
A SYMBOL OF HIS POWER,
A BIGGER PHALLIC SYMBOL
THAN A PORSCHE.
VICTORIA BILLINGS

this is page
37

"LOVE"

IT'S NOT THE MEN IN MY LIFE THAT COUNTS
– IT'S THE LIFE IN MY MEN.

MAE WEST

I LOVE THE MALE BODY. IT'S BETTER DESIGNED THAN THE MALE MIND.

ANDREA NEWMAN

A girl can wait for the right man to come along,
but in the meantime that still doesn't mean
she can't have a wonderful time
with all the wrong ones.

CHER

Lead me not into temptation;
I can find the way myself.

RITA MAE BROWN

"What's Love Got To Do With It?"

**IT'S THE GOOD GIRLS WHO KEEP DIARIES;
THE BAD GIRLS NEVER HAVE THE TIME.**
TALLULAH BANKHEAD

Women might be able to fake orgasms,
but men can fake a whole relationship.
SHARON STONE

Sex at 93 is like
playing billiards
with a rope.
GEORGE BURNS

MEN WANT THE SAME THING
FROM THEIR UNDERWEAR THAT
THEY WANT FROM WOMEN:
A LITTLE BIT OF SUPPORT,
AND A LITTLE BIT OF FREEDOM.
JERRY SEINFELD

**I'll come to your room at eight o'clock.
If I'm late, start without me.**

TALLULAH BANKHEAD

*A man can sleep around, no questions asked,
but if a woman makes 19 or 20 mistakes
she's a tramp.*

JOAN RIVERS

I can still enjoy sex at 75.
I live at 76, so it's no distance.

BOB MONKHOUSE

I wasn't kissing her.
I was just whispering
in her mouth.

CHICO MARX

"What's Love Got To Do With It?"

I HAVE EVERYTHING NOW
THAT I HAD 20 YEARS AGO
– EXCEPT NOW IT'S ALL LOWER.
GYPSY ROSE LEE

It's hard to be naked
and not be upstaged
by your nipples.
SUSAN SARANDON

My brain?
It's my second favourite organ.
WOODY ALLEN

WOMEN SHOULD BE OBSCENE AND NOT HEARD.
GROUCHO MARX

"LOVE"

I wonder why men can get serious at all.
They have this delicate long thing hanging
outside their bodies, which goes up and
down by its own will ... if I were a man
I would always be laughing at myself.

YOKO ONO

If the world were a logical place, men would ride sidesaddle.

RITA MAE BROWN

The average man is more interested
in a woman who is interested in him
than in a woman – any woman
– with beautiful legs.

MARLENE DIETRICH

I GENERALLY AVOID TEMPTATION UNLESS I CAN'T RESIST IT.

MAE WEST

"Love and Marriage"

Place me like a seal over your heart,
like a seal on your arm;
for love is as strong as death,
its jealousy unyielding as the grave.
It burns like blazing fire,
like a mighty flame.
Many waters cannot quench love;
rivers cannot wash it away.
If one were to give all the wealth
of his house for love,
it would be utterly scorned.

THE BIBLE (SONG OF SOLOMON)

Wedlock is the deep, deep peace of the double bed
after the hurly-burly of the chaise longue.

MRS PATRICK CAMPBELL

INTIMACY IS WHAT
MAKES A MARRIAGE,
NOT A CEREMONY,
NOT A PIECE OF PAPER
FROM THE STATE.

KATHLEEN NORRIS

this is page
43

"LOVE"

My advice to you is get married:
if you find a good wife you'll be happy;
if not, you'll become a philosopher.

SOCRATES

Will you marry me?
Did he leave you any money?
Answer the second question first.

GROUCHO MARX

It's not a good idea
to put your wife into a novel;
not your latest wife anyway.

NORMAN MAILER

MARRIAGE IS JUST THE FIRST STEP
TOWARDS DIVORCE.

ZSA ZSA GABOR

"Love and Marriage"

**I USED TO BELIEVE THAT MARRIAGE
WOULD DIMINISH ME, REDUCE MY OPTIONS.
THAT YOU HAD TO BE SOMEONE LESS
TO LIVE WITH SOMEONE ELSE WHEN,
OF COURSE, YOU HAVE TO BE SOMEONE MORE.**

CANDICE BERGEN

Matrimony:
friendship under
difficult circumstances.

ROSE SCOTT

My boyfriend and I broke up.
He wanted to get married
and I didn't want him to.

RITA RUDNER

Marriage is a wonderful invention.
But then again, so is a bicycle repair kit.

BILLY CONNOLLY

"LOVE"

**A man would often be the lover of his wife
if he were married to someone else.**

ELINOR GLYN

In a marriage, it takes just one to make a quarrel.

OGDEN NASH

It's impossible to live at peace
with anyone you love.
You can only live at peace
with those to whom you are indifferent.

MARTIN BOYD

That married couples can
live together day after day
is one miracle the Vatican
has overlooked.

BILL COSBY

"Love and Marriage"

**I FEEL SURE THAT NO GIRL WOULD
GO TO THE ALTAR IF SHE KNEW ALL.**

QUEEN VICTORIA

Never go to bed mad.
Stay up and fight.

PHYLLIS DILLER

In every marriage more than a week old,
there are grounds for divorce.
The trick is to find, and continue to find,
grounds for marriage.

ROBERT ANDERSON

**I HAD BAD LUCK WITH BOTH MY WIVES.
THE FIRST ONE LEFT ME
AND THE SECOND ONE DIDN'T.**

BOB MONKHOUSE

"LOVE"

My wife and I were happy for 20 years. Then we met.
RODNEY DANGERFIELD

It seemed to me that the desire to get married – which,
I regret to say, I believe is basic and primal in women
– is followed almost immediately by an equally basic
and primal urge – which is to be single again.

NORA EPHRON

The married are those who have taken the
terrible risk of intimacy and, having taken it,
know life without intimacy to be impossible.

CAROLYN G. HEILBRUN

The majority of husbands remind me of an orangutan trying to play the violin.

HONORÉ DE BALZAC

"Love and Marriage"

**THE BEST WAY TO GET HUSBANDS TO DO SOMETHING
IS TO SUGGEST THAT THEY ARE TOO OLD TO DO IT.**
SHIRLEY MACLAINE

The conception of two people living together
for twenty-five years without having a
cross word suggests a lack of spirit
only to be admired in sheep.
ALAN PATRICK HERBERT

*Strange to say what delight
we married people have to see these
poor fools decoyed into our condition.*
SAMUEL PEPYS

**MOST WIVES THINK OF THEIR HUSBANDS
AS BUMBLING BRAGGARTS WITH
WHOM THEY HAPPEN TO BE IN LOVE.**
JACKIE GLEASON

"LOVE"

What ought to be done
to the man who invented
the celebrating of anniversaries?
Mere killing would be too light.

MARK TWAIN

Chumps always make the best husbands.
When you marry, Sally, grab a chump.

P.G. WODEHOUSE

Keep your eyes wide open before
marriage, half shut afterwards.

BENJAMIN FRANKLIN

Never feel remorse for
what you've thought about your
wife, for she's thought much
worse things about you.

JEAN ROSTAND

"Love and Marriage"

**IN A TWO-CAR FAMILY,
THE WIFE ALWAYS HAS THE SMALLER CAR.**
RUTH RENDELL

On quiet nights, when I'm alone,
I like to run our wedding video backwards
just so that I can watch myself walking out
of the church a free man.
JIM DAVIDSON

*I married beneath me,
all women do.*
NANCY ASTOR

**WHY BUY A BOOK WHEN YOU CAN
JOIN THE LIBRARY?**
LILY SAVAGE

"LOVE"

A happy marriage is the world's best bargain.

O.A. BATTISTA

There is more to marriage than
four bare legs under a blanket.

ROBERTSON DAVIES

An archaeologist is the best husband
a woman can have; the older she gets
the more interested he is in her.

AGATHA CHRISTIE

*I believe in the institution
of marriage, and I intend to
keep trying till I get it right.*

RICHARD PRYOR

"Love and Marriage"

DO NOT ADULTERY COMMIT;
ADVANTAGE RARELY COMES OF IT.
ARTHUR HUGH CLOUGH

A wedding is like a funeral
where you can smell your own flowers.
EDDIE CANTOR

Adultery is the application
of democracy to love.
H.L. MENCKEN

EVERY MODERN MALE HAS, LYING AT THE BOTTOM
OF HIS PSYCHE, A LARGE, PRIMITIVE BEING COVERED
WITH HAIR DOWN TO HIS FEET. MAKING CONTACT
WITH THIS WILD MAN IS THE STEP THE 80S MAN OR
THE 90S MAN HAS YET TO TAKE.
ROBERT BLY

"LOVE"

Yes, my husband is younger than me,
but it's not a problem. If he dies, he dies.

JOAN COLLINS

No nice men are good
at getting taxis.

KATHARINE WHITEHORN

It is a universally accepted truth
that a single man in possession of a
good fortune must be in want of a wife.

JANE AUSTEN

I married a few people
I shouldn't have . . .
but haven't we all?

MAMIE VAN DOREN

"Love and Marriage"

IF YOU WOULD UNDERSTAND MEN, STUDY WOMEN.

FRENCH PROVERB

A man who has nothing to do with women
is always incomplete.

CYRIL CONNOLLY

The male is a domestic animal
which, if treated with firmness,
can be trained to do most things.

JILLY COOPER

CAN YOU IMAGINE A WORLD WITHOUT MEN?
NO CRIME AND LOTS OF HAPPY FAT WOMEN.

NICOLE HOLLANDER

"LOVE"

MEN SHOULD BE LIKE KLEENEX – SOFT, STRONG AND DISPOSABLE.

CHER

People think at the end of the day that a man is the only answer. Actually a job is better for me.

DIANA, PRINCESS OF WALES

The great question that has never been answered,
and which I have not yet been able to answer,
despite my 30 years of research into the feminine soul,
is 'What does a woman want?'

SIGMUND FREUD

WOMEN ARE LIKE ELEPHANTS TO ME: NICE TO LOOK AT, BUT I WOULDN'T WANT TO OWN ONE.

W.C. FIELDS

"Love and Marriage"

It's the women who make decisions. Women are strong, women are the doers, that's the way it is.

EUGENIE CLARK

SOME OF US ARE BECOMING THE MEN WE WANTED TO MARRY.

GLORIA STEINEM

I am a woman meant for a man, but I never found a man who could compete.

BETTE DAVIS

The female of the species is more deadly than the male.

RUDYARD KIPLING

"LOVE"

*In societies where men
are truly confident of their own worth,
women are not merely tolerated but valued.*
AUNG SAN SUU KYI

Friendship can only exist between persons with
similar interests and points of view. Man and woman
by the conventions of society are born with different
interests and different points of view.
AUGUST STRINDBERG

Women have very little idea
of how much men hate them.
GERMAINE GREER

Women deprived of
the company of men pine,
men deprived of the company of women
become stupid.
ANTON CHEKHOV

"Love and Marriage"

Nagging is the repetition of unpalatable truths.

EDITH SUMMERSKILL

There are times when even
a dedicated feminist needs
a chauvinist to lean on.

CLIVE CUSSLER

*A man who correctly guesses a woman's age
may be smart, but he's not very bright.*

LUCILLE BALL

*The first problem for all of us,
men and women, is not to learn
but to unlearn.*

GLORIA STEINEM

"LOVE"

A man's brain has a more difficult time shifting from thinking to feeling than a woman's brain does.

BARBARA DE ANGELIS

It is better to be unfaithful than faithful without wanting to be.

BRIGITTE BARDOT

MEN KICK FRIENDSHIP ROUND LIKE A FOOTBALL AND IT DOESN'T SEEM TO CRACK. WOMEN TREAT IT LIKE GLASS AND IT GOES TO PIECES.

ANON

Women want mediocre men, and men are working hard to become as mediocre as possible.

MARGARET MEAD

"Love and Marriage"

Most women set out
to try to change a man, and
when they have changed him
they do not like him.

MARLENE DIETRICH

*Nobody will ever win the battle
of the sexes. There's too much
fraternising with the enemy.*

HENRY KISSINGER

A woman without a man is like
a fish without a bicycle.

GLORIA STEINEM

*THE ONLY TIME A WOMAN REALLY
SUCCEEDS IN CHANGING A MAN
IS WHEN HE'S A BABY.*

NATALIE WOOD

"LOVE"

SIR, IF YOU WERE MY HUSBAND,
I'D POISON YOUR TEA.

LADY ASTOR TO WINSTON CHURCHILL

MADAM, IF YOU WERE MY WIFE,
I'D DRINK IT.

WINSTON CHURCHILL TO LADY ASTOR

All women become
like their mothers.
That is their tragedy.
No man does. That's his.

OSCAR WILDE

A relationship, I think, is like a shark,
you know? It has to constantly move
forward or it dies. And I think what we
got on our hands is a dead shark.

WOODY ALLEN

THE FORMULA FOR ACHIEVING
A SUCCESSFUL RELATIONSHIP IS SIMPLE:
YOU SHOULD TREAT ALL DISASTERS
AS IF THEY WERE TRIVIALITIES BUT
NEVER TREAT A TRIVIALITY
AS IF IT WERE A DISASTER.

QUENTIN CRISP

*A successful marriage requires falling in love
many times, always with the same person.*

MIGNON MCLAUGHLIN

Come live with me and be my love,
And we will some new pleasures prove
Of golden sands and crystal brooks,
With silken lines and silver hooks.

JOHN DONNE

"LOVE"

God, the best maker of all marriages,
Combine your hearts into one.
WILLIAM SHAKESPEARE

What greater thing is there for two human souls,
than to feel that they are joined for life – to
strengthen each other in all labour, to rest on each
other in all sorrow, to minister to each other in all
pain, to be one with each other in silent unspeakable
memories at the moment of the last parting?
GEORGE ELIOT

MARRIAGE IS NOT A NOUN; IT'S A VERB.
IT ISN'T SOMETHING YOU GET.
IT'S SOMETHING YOU DO.
IT'S THE WAY YOU LOVE
YOUR PARTNER EVERY DAY.
BARBARA DE ANGELIS

"Love and Marriage"

A GREAT MARRIAGE IS NOT WHEN THE
'PERFECT COUPLE' COMES TOGETHER. IT
IS WHEN AN IMPERFECT COUPLE LEARNS
TO ENJOY THEIR DIFFERENCES.

DAVE MEURER

Let all thy joys be as the month of May,
And all thy days be as a marriage day.

FRANCIS QUARLES

Basically, my wife was immature.
I'd be at home taking a bath and
she'd come in and sink my boats.

WOODY ALLEN

Any intelligent woman who reads the marriage contract
and then goes into it, deserves all the consequences.

ISADORA DUNCAN

"LOVE"

A single man has not nearly the value he would have in a state of union. He is an incomplete animal. He resembles the odd half of a pair of scissors.

BENJAMIN FRANKLIN

Bachelors have consciences, married men have wives.

SAMUEL JOHNSON

I DON'T THINK MY WIFE LIKES ME VERY MUCH. WHEN I HAD A HEART ATTACK, SHE WROTE FOR AN AMBULANCE.

FRANK CARSON

I love being married.
It's so great to find that
one special person you want to
annoy for the rest of your life.

RITA RUDNER

"Love and Marriage"

Love one another and you will be happy.
It's as simple and as difficult as that.
MICHAEL LEUNIG

My wife told me I'd drive her to her grave.
I had the car out in two minutes.
TOMMY COOPER

*MARRIAGE IS POPULAR BECAUSE
IT COMBINES THE MAXIMUM OF TEMPTATION
WITH THE MAXIMUM OF OPPORTUNITY.*
GEORGE BERNARD SHAW

A man doesn't know what
happiness is until he's married.
By then it's too late.
FRANK SINATRA

"LOVE"

Let there be spaces in your togetherness and
let the winds of the heavens dance between you.
Love one another but make not a bond of love:
let it rather be a moving sea between the shores
of your souls. Fill each other's cup,
but drink not from one cup.

KAHLIL GIBRAN

There is in marriage an energy and an impulse of joy
that lasts as long as life and that survives all sorts
of suffering and distress and weariness. The triumph of
marriage over all its antagonists is almost inexplicable.

JAMES DOUGLAS

TWO HUMAN LOVES
MAKE ONE DIVINE.

ELIZABETH BARRETT BROWNING

" FAMILY "

The family is
the homeland
of the heart.

GIUSEPPE
MAZZINI

"When a Child is Born"

A baby is God's opinion that the world should go on.
CARL SANDBURG

It is not advisable to put your head around your child's door to see if it is asleep. It was.
FAITH HINES

A child is helpless in inverse proportion to his age.
He is at the zenith of his powers while he is an infant in arms.
What on earth is more powerful than a very young baby?
ALINE KILMER

"When a Child is Born"

OUR BIRTH IS NOTHING BUT OUR DEATH BEGUN.
EDWARD YOUNG

Don't parents get blamed too much
for over-influencing their children,
when the blame should mostly lie on
the children for not kicking more
strenuously against their influence?
C.E. MONTAGUE

Somewhere in the world, every ten seconds,
there is a woman giving birth to a child.
She must be found and stopped.
SAM LEVESON

I COULD NOT POINT TO ANY NEED IN CHILDHOOD AS
STRONG AS THAT FOR A FATHER'S PROTECTION.
SIGMUND FREUD

"FAMILY"

Better to play 15 minutes enjoyably
and then say, 'Now I'm going to read my paper'
than to spend all day at the zoo crossly.
DR BENJAMIN SPOCK

Every child is an artist.
The problem is how to remain
an artist once he grows up.
PABLO PICASSO

Contraceptives should be used on
every conceivable occasion.
SPIKE MILLIGAN

If you want to see what children can do,
you must stop giving them things.
NORMAN DOUGLAS

A TWO YEAR OLD IS KIND OF LIKE HAVING A BLENDER,
BUT YOU DON'T HAVE A TOP FOR IT.

JERRY SEINFELD

I got married and we had a baby
nine months and ten seconds later.

JAYNE MANSFIELD

Children need love,
especially when they do not deserve it.

HAROLD S. HULBERT

A BABY IS NOTHING MORE THAN
A LOUD NOISE AT ONE END AND
NO SENSE OF RESPONSIBILITY
AT THE OTHER.

RONALD KNOX

"FAMILY"

IT TAKES THREE TO MAKE A BIRTHDAY.
PENELOPE LEACH

Giving birth is like taking your lower lip
and forcing it over your head.
CAROL BURNETT

Death and taxes and childbirth.
There's never any convenient
time for any of them!
MARGARET MITCHELL

When your first baby drops
its dummy, you sterilise it.
When your second baby drops its
dummy, you tell the dog to fetch.
BRUCE LANSKY

"When a Child is Born"

**ALL BABIES ARE SUPPOSED TO LOOK LIKE ME
– AT BOTH ENDS.**

WINSTON CHURCHILL

Good work, Mary.
We all knew you had it in you.

DOROTHY PARKER

Don't buy one of those baby monitors.
Babies pretend to be dead.
They're bastards and they do it
on purpose.

BILLY CONNOLLY

**IF MEN HAD TO HAVE BABIES, THEY
WOULD ONLY EVER HAVE ONE EACH.**

DIANA, PRINCESS OF WALES

No matter what the ordinary person says,
no matter who it is that speaks,
or what superlatives are employed,
no baby is admired sufficiently to please the mother.
E.V. LUCAS

Babies are amazing. The way they stare into your eyes,
their exuberant smiles, how they begin each day all warm
and sleepy, smelling of promise. I suppose I never realised
it before, babies aren't really born of their parents,
they're born of every kind word, loving gesture,
hope and dream their parents ever had. Bliss.
JULIA ROBERTS

The first child is made of glass,
the second porcelain, the rest
of rubber, steel and granite.
RICHARD J. NEEDHAM

"When a Child is Born"

No phallic hero, no matter what he does to himself or to another to prove his courage, ever matches the solitary, existential courage of the woman who gives birth.

ANDREA DWORKIN

People who say they sleep like a baby usually don't have one.

LEO J. BURKE

By far the most common craving of pregnant women is not to be pregnant.

PHYLLIS DILLER

THERE NEVER WAS A CHILD SO LOVELY BUT HIS MOTHER WAS GLAD TO GET ASLEEP.

RALPH WALDO EMERSON

"FAMILY"

What is a home without children? Quiet.

HENNY YOUNGMAN

For a father, a home birth is preferable.
That way you're not missing
anything on television.

JEREMY HARDY

Humans are the only animals
that have children on purpose –
with the exception of guppies,
who like to eat theirs.

P.J. O'ROURKE

My husband and I have decided to
start a family while my parents are still
young enough to look after them.

RITA RUDNER

"When a Child is Born"

**WHEN I WAS A CHILD, I SPAKE AS A CHILD,
I UNDERSTOOD AS A CHILD, I THOUGHT AS A CHILD:
BUT WHEN I BECAME A MAN,
I PUT AWAY CHILDISH THINGS.**

THE BIBLE (I CORINTHIANS)

Parents can only give good advice or put on the right paths, but the final forming of a person's character lies in their own hands.

ANNE FRANK

I love children . . . if they're properly cooked.

W.C. FIELDS

**THE QUICKEST WAY FOR A PARENT
TO GET A CHILD'S ATTENTION IS TO
SIT DOWN AND LOOK COMFORTABLE.**

LANE OLINGHOUSE

"FAMILY"

**Children should be seen
and not smelt.**

JOYCE JILLSON

Don't have any children.
It makes divorce so much more complicated.

ALBERT EINSTEIN

THE REAL MENACE IN DEALING
WITH A FIVE YEAR OLD IS THAT IN
NO TIME AT ALL YOU BEGIN TO
SOUND LIKE A FIVE YEAR OLD.

JEAN KERR

Adam and Eve had many advantages,
but the principal one was that they
escaped teething.

MARK TWAIN

"When a Child is Born"

NEVER HAVE IDEAS ABOUT CHILDREN, AND NEVER HAVE IDEAS FOR THEM.

GEORGE ORWELL

I love to go down to the playground and
watch all the children jumping and shouting.
They don't know that I'm firing blanks.

EMO PHILIPS

*The trouble with children is that
they are not returnable.*

QUENTIN CRISP

EVERYONE HAD AN UNCLE WHO TRIED TO STEAL THEIR NOSE.

PETER KAY

"FAMILY"

There is no end to the violations committed by children on children, quietly talking alone.
ELIZABETH BOWEN

FATHERHOOD IS PRETENDING
THE PRESENT THAT YOU LOVE MOST
IS SOAP ON A ROPE.
BILL COSBY

The hardest job kids face today
is learning good manners
without seeing any.
FRED ASTAIRE

If you desire to drain to the dregs the fullest cup of scorn
and hatred that a fellow human being can pour out for
you, let a young mother hear you call her baby 'it'.
JEROME K. JEROME

"When a Child is Born"

**IF THERE IS ANYTHING THAT WE WISH TO CHANGE
IN A CHILD, WE SHOULD FIRST EXAMINE IT AND SEE
WHETHER IT IS NOT SOMETHING THAT COULD
BETTER BE CHANGED IN OURSELVES.**

CARL JUNG

There's this myth that, as a father, if you are
there at the birth, you're sharing the birthing
experience. Unless you're opening an umbrella
up your ass, I don't think so.

ROBIN WILLIAMS

*I've never outgrown that feeling
of mild pride of acceptance,
when children take your hand.*

IAN MCEWAN

"FAMILY"

When childhood dies, its corpses are called adults.
BRIAN ALDISS

I love children, especially
when they cry, because then
somebody takes them away.
NANCY MITFORD

Watching your daughter being collected
by her date feels like handing over a
$1 million Stradivarius to a gorilla.
JIM BISHOP

A HAPPY CHILDHOOD
HAS SPOILED MANY
A PROMISING LIFE.
ROBERTSON DAVIES

"When a Child is Born"

**WHAT MUSIC IS MORE ENCHANTING
THAN THE VOICES OF YOUNG PEOPLE,
WHEN YOU CAN'T HEAR WHAT THEY SAY?**
LOGAN PEARSALL SMITH

You know that children are growing up when
they start asking questions that have answers.
JOHN J. PLOMP

When I was born I was so surprised
that I didn't talk for a year and a half.
GRACIE ALLEN

**ONE OF THE MOST OBVIOUS FACTS ABOUT
GROWNUPS TO A CHILD IS THAT THEY HAVE
FORGOTTEN WHAT IT IS LIKE TO BE A CHILD.**
RANDALL JARRELL

"FAMILY"

**Children are not things to be moulded,
but are people to be unfolded.**

JESS LAIR

When I was a kid my parents moved a lot,
but I always found them.

RODNEY DANGERFIELD

A child is not a vase to be filled,
but a fire to be lit.

FRANÇOIS RABELAIS

IF I EVER HAD TWINS,
I'D USE ONE FOR PARTS.

STEVEN WRIGHT

A mother never realises that her children
are no longer children.

HOLBROOK JACKSON

I was so ugly when I was born that
the doctor slapped my mother.

HENRY YOUNGMAN

NO MAN CAN POSSIBLY KNOW WHAT LIFE MEANS,
WHAT THE WORLD MEANS, WHAT ANYTHING MEANS,
UNTIL HE HAS A CHILD AND LOVES IT.

LAFCADIO HEARN

My mother hated me. She once took me
to an orphanage and told me to mingle.

JOAN RIVERS

"FAMILY"

**LEVEL WITH YOUR CHILD BY BEING HONEST.
NOBODY SPOTS A PHONY QUICKER THAN A CHILD.**
MARY MACCRACKEN

*The trouble with children is
that they are not returnable.*
QUENTIN CRISP

Grown-ups never understand anything for themselves,
and it is tiresome for children to be always and
forever explaining things to them.
ANTOINE DE SAINT-EXUPÉRY

If thine enemy offend thee,
give his child a drum.
FRAN LIEBOWITZ

"When a Child is Born"

IT DOESN'T MATTER WHO MY FATHER WAS;
IT MATTERS WHO I REMEMBER HE WAS.
ANNE SEXTON

Everyone wants to save the Earth.
No one wants to help Mom dry the dishes.
P.J. O'ROURKE

As is the mother,
so is her daughter.
THE BIBLE (EZEKIEL)

IF YOU MUST HOLD YOURSELF UP
TO YOUR CHILDREN AS AN OBJECT LESSON
(WHICH IS NOT AT ALL NECESSARY),
HOLD YOURSELF UP AS A WARNING
AND NOT AS AN EXAMPLE.
GEORGE BERNARD SHAW

"FAMILY"

Whatever else is unsure in this stinking dunghill of a world a mother's love is not.

JAMES JOYCE

NEVER LEND YOUR CAR TO ANYONE TO WHOM YOU HAVE GIVEN BIRTH.

NORA EPHRON

NEVER HELP A CHILD WITH A TASK AT WHICH HE FEELS HE CAN SUCCEED.

MARIA MONTESSORI

If you bungle raising your children, I don't think whatever else you do matters very much.

JACKIE KENNEDY ONASSIS

"When a Child is Born"

**MY MOTHER LOVED CHILDREN
– SHE WOULD HAVE GIVEN ANYTHING
IF I'D BEEN ONE.**

GROUCHO MARX

Adults are just obsolete children.

DR SEUSS

Motherhood is like sex and death;
you can't imagine it until you do it.
It's completely overwhelming,
all-else obliterating passion
for a little blob!

JULIET STEVENSON

**THE THING THAT BEST DEFINES A CHILD
IS THE TOTAL INABILITY TO ABSORB INFORMATION
FROM ANYTHING NOT PLUGGED IN.**

BILL COSBY

THERE IS NO MORE SOMBRE ENEMY OF GOOD ART
THAN THE PRAM IN THE HALL.

CYRIL CONNOLLY

Even when freshly washed and
relieved of all obvious confections,
children tend to be sticky.

FRAN LIEBOWITZ

In our society ... mothers go on
getting blamed until they're 80,
but shouldn't take it personally.

BARBARA CARTLAND

The reason grandparents and
grandchildren get along so well is
that they have a common enemy.

SAM LEVENSON

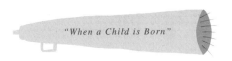

 "When a Child is Born"

*I have only two rules for
my newly born daughter.
She will dress well;
she will never have sex.*

JOHN MALKOVICH

**Facing a mirror you see merely your own countenance;
facing your child you finally understand
how everyone else has seen you.**

DANIEL RAEBURN

Having one child makes you a parent;
having two you are a referee.

DAVID FROST

LITTLE GIRLS ARE CUTE AND SMALL
ONLY TO ADULTS. TO ONE ANOTHER
THEY ARE NOT CUTE. THEY ARE LIFE-SIZED.

MARGARET ATWOOD

"FAMILY"

Father and son are natural enemies and each is happier and more secure in keeping it that way.

JOHN STEINBECK

Adults are always asking little kids what they want to be when they grow up because they're looking for ideas.

PAULA POUNDSTONE

I have four sons and three stepsons. I have learnt what it is like to step on Lego with bare feet.

FAY WELDON

Children are the world's most valuable resource and its best hope for the future.

JOHN F. KENNEDY

"When a Child is Born"

SHE GOT HER LOOKS FROM HER FATHER.
HE'S A PLASTIC SURGEON.
GROUCHO MARX

Let us put our minds together
and see what life we can make
for our children.
SITTING BULL

There are two things in life for which
we are never truly prepared: twins.
JOSH BILLINGS

HE WHO TEACHES CHILDREN
LEARNS MORE THAN THEY DO.
GERMAN PROVERB

"We Are Family"

EVERY LARGE FAMILY HAS ITS ANGEL AND ITS DEMON.
JOSEPH ROUX

There's nothing wrong with teenagers that reasoning with them won't aggravate.
JEAN KERR

Family, nature and health all go together.
OLIVIA NEWTON-JOHN

"We Are Family"

AS TO THE FAMILY, I HAVE NEVER UNDERSTOOD WHY IT SHOULD
BE AN IDEAL AT ALL. A GROUP OF CLOSELY RELATED PERSONS,
LIVING UNDER ONE ROOF; IT IS A CONVENIENCE, OFTEN A
NECESSITY, SOMETIMES A PLEASURE, SOMETIMES THE REVERSE;
BUT WHO FIRST EXALTED IT AS ADMIRABLE?

ROSE MACAULAY

A women should be home with the children,
building that home and making sure
there's a secure family atmosphere.

MEL GIBSON

Where does the family start? It starts with
a young man falling in love with a girl. No
superior alternative has yet been found.

WINSTON CHURCHILL

YOU DON'T CHOOSE YOUR FAMILY.
THEY ARE GOD'S GIFT TO YOU AS YOU ARE TO THEM.

DESMOND TUTU

"FAMILY"

**All happy families are alike;
each unhappy family is unhappy in its own way.**

LEO TOLSTOY

The happiness of the domestic fireside
is the first boon of Heaven; and it is well
it is so, since it is that which is the lot of
the mass of mankind.

THOMAS JEFFERSON

THERE IS NO SUCH THING AS
'FUN FOR THE WHOLE FAMILY'.

JERRY SEINFELD

When your relatives are at home,
we have to think of all their good points
or it would be impossible to endure them.

GEORGE BERNARD SHAW

"We Are Family"

**EVERY MAN SEES IN HIS RELATIVES,
AND ESPECIALLY IN HIS COUSINS,
A SERIES OF GROTESQUE CARICATURES OF HIMSELF.**
H.L. MENCKEN

The great advantage of living in a large family
is that early lesson of life's essential unfairness.
NANCY MITFORD

Without a family, man,
alone in the world,
trembles with the cold.
ANDRÉ MAUROIS

TO THE FAMILY – THAT DEAR OCTOPUS FROM
WHOSE TENTACLES WE NEVER QUITE ESCAPE NOR,
IN OUR INMOST HEARTS, EVER QUITE WISH TO.
DODIE SMITH

"FAMILY"

The happiest moments of my life have been
the few which I have passed at home
in the bosom of my family.

THOMAS JEFFERSON

*A family's photograph album is generally
about the extended family – and, often,
is all that remains of it.*

SUSAN SONTAG

Families are about love
overcoming emotional torture.

MATT GROENING

Dad kept us out of school,
but school comes and goes.
Family is forever.

CHARLIE SHEEN

"We Are Family"

PARENTS SHOULD CONDUCT THEIR ARGUMENTS IN QUIET, RESPECTFUL TONES, BUT IN A FOREIGN LANGUAGE. YOU'D BE SURPRISED WHAT AN INDUCEMENT THAT IS TO THE EDUCATION OF CHILDREN.

JUDITH MARTIN

Fathers should neither be seen nor heard. That is the only proper basis for family life.

OSCAR WILDE

No one but doctors and mothers know what it means to have interruptions.

KARL A. MENNINGER

A MAN SHOULD NEVER NEGLECT HIS FAMILY FOR BUSINESS.

WALT DISNEY

"FAMILY"

Family quarrels are bitter things. They don't go according to any rules. They're not like aches or wounds; they're more like splits in the skin that won't heal because there's not enough material.

F. SCOTT FITZGERALD

All the men in my family were bearded . . . and most of the women.

W.C. FIELDS

No matter how many communes anybody invents, the family always creeps back.

MARGARET MEAD

As the family goes, so goes the nation and so goes the whole world in which we live.

POPE JOHN PAUL II

"We Are Family"

FAR FROM BEING THE BASIS OF THE GOOD SOCIETY, THE FAMILY, WITH ITS NARROW PRIVACY AND TAWDRY SECRETS, IS THE SOURCE OF ALL OUR DISCONTENTS.
EDMUND LEACH

Family love is messy, clinging, and of an annoying and repetitive pattern, like bad wallpaper.
P.J. O'ROURKE

She knew one of the great family truths, that aunts always help, while moms always think it would be good for you if you did it yourself.
JANE SMILEY

I CANNOT REMEMBER A MOMENT IN MY LIFE WHEN I HAVE NOT FELT THE LOVE OF MY FAMILY. WE WERE A FAMILY THAT WOULD HAVE KILLED FOR EACH OTHER, AND WE STILL ARE.
RICHARD BRANSON

"FAMILY"

I am the family face;
Flesh perishes, I live on,
Projecting trait and trace
Through time to times anon …
THOMAS HARDY

*THERE'S NO ROAD MAP ON
HOW TO RAISE A FAMILY:
IT'S ALWAYS AN ENORMOUS
NEGOTIATION.*
MERYL STREEP

The human being cannot live too long
in the infantile environment,
that is, in the bosom of his family,
without serious danger to his psychic health.
CARL JUNG

"We Are Family"

**LIKE ALL THE BEST FAMILIES,
WE HAVE OUR SHARE OF ECCENTRICITIES,
OF IMPETUOUS AND WAYWARD YOUNGSTERS
AND OF FAMILY DISAGREEMENTS.**
QUEEN ELIZABETH II

Family ... the home of all social evil,
a charitable institution for comfortable women,
an anchorage for house-fathers
and a hell for children.
AUGUST STRINDBERG

Family jokes, though rightly cursed
by strangers, are the bond
that keeps most families alive.
STELLA BENSON

**HAPPINESS IS HAVING A LARGE, LOVING,
CARING, CLOSE-KNIT FAMILY
IN ANOTHER CITY.**
GEORGE BURNS

"FAMILY"

Call it a clan, call it a network, call it a tribe, call it a family.
Whatever you call it, whoever you are, you need one.
JANE HOWARD

I'm a girl from a good family
who was very well brought up.
One day I turned my back on it all
and became a bohemian.
BRIGITTE BARDOT

A brother is a friend given by Nature.
GABRIEL MARIE LEGOUVÉ

ACTING IS JUST A WAY OF MAKING
A LIVING. THE FAMILY IS LIFE.
DENZEL WASHINGTON

"We Are Family"

**THE AWE AND DREAD WITH WHICH THE UNTUTORED SAVAGE
CONTEMPLATES HIS MOTHER-IN-LAW ARE AMONGST
THE MOST FAMILIAR FACTS OF ANTHROPOLOGY.**

JAMES G. FRAZER

I have frequently been questioned, especially by women, of how I could reconcile family life with a scientific career. Well, it has not been easy.

MARIE CURIE

All American films boil down to
'I love you, Dad ...'

IAN HISLOP

**I HAVE BEEN CALLED
A NUN WITH A SWITCHBLADE
WHERE MY PRIVACY IS CONCERNED.
I THINK THERE'S A POINT WHERE
ONE SAYS, THAT'S FOR FAMILY,
THAT'S FOR ME.**

JULIE ANDREWS

"FAMILY"

The most remarkable thing about my mother is that for 30 years she served the family nothing but leftovers. The original meal has never been found.

CALVIN TRILLIN

Sometimes you struggle so hard to feed your family one way, you forget to feed them the other way, with spiritual nourishment. Everybody needs that.

JAMES BROWN

Cleaning your house while your kids are still growing is like shovelling the walk before it stops snowing.

PHYLLIS DILLER

If you cannot get rid of the family skeleton, you may as well make it dance.

GEORGE BERNARD SHAW

"We Are Family"

*IT'S ODD HOW ALL MEN DEVELOP THE NOTION,
AS THEY GROW OLDER, THAT THEIR MOTHERS WERE
WONDERFUL COOKS. I HAVE YET TO MEET A MAN
WHO WILL ADMIT THAT HIS MOTHER WAS A
KITCHEN ASSASSIN AND NEARLY POISONED HIM.*

ROBERTSON DAVIES

**To us, family means putting your arms
around each other and being there.**

BARBARA BUSH

Setting a good example for children
takes all the fun out of middle age.

WILLIAM FEATHER

FAMILY IS NOT AN IMPORTANT THING,
IT'S EVERYTHING.

MICHAEL J. FOX

"Together Forever"

There is more difference within the sexes than between them.

IVY COMPTON-BURNETT

NOT ONLY IS IT HARDER TO BE A MAN, IT IS HARDER TO BECOME ONE.

ARIANNA HUFFINGTON

THERE WAS NEVER A GREAT MAN WHO HAD NOT A GREAT MOTHER.

OLIVE SCHREINER

"Together Forever"

**A WOMAN IS LIKE A TEA BAG – YOU NEVER KNOW
HOW STRONG SHE IS UNTIL SHE GETS IN HOT WATER.**
ELEANOR ROOSEVELT

Behind every famous man is a woman who says
there is a woman behind every famous man.
HAL ROACH

I am all for women's rights . . . and their lefts, too.
GROUCHO MARX

**THE MALE SEX STILL CONSTITUTE
IN MANY WAYS THE MOST OBSTINATE
VESTED INTEREST ONE CAN FIND.**
LORD LONGFORD

"FAMILY"

**DON'T ACCEPT RIDES FROM STRANGE MEN,
AND REMEMBER THAT ALL MEN ARE STRANGE.**
ROBIN MORGAN

*I am not a do-gooder.
I am a revolutionary.
A revolutionary woman.*
JANE FONDA

I did everything that Fred Astaire did,
except I did it backwards and in high heels.
GINGER ROGERS

When once a woman has given you
her heart, you can never get rid
of the rest of her body.
JOHN VANBRUGH

"Together Forever"

*I think the key is for women
not to set any limits.*
MARTINA NAVRATILOVA

They say a woman's work is never done.
All I'm saying is, maybe if you organised
yourselves a bit better . . .
JIMMY CARR

Once a man is on hand,
a woman tends to stop believing
in her own beliefs.
COLETTE DOWLING

WHEREAS NATURE TURNS GIRLS INTO WOMEN,
SOCIETY HAS TO MAKE BOYS INTO MEN.
ANTHONY STEVENS

"FAMILY"

Men are all the same. They always think that something they are going to get is better than what they have got.

JOHN OLIVER HOBBES

Someone has to stand up for wimps.

BARBARA EHRENREICH

When a woman says she wants to go out and get a job to express herself, it usually means that she's hopelessly behind with the ironing.

OLIVER REED

SO FEW GROWN WOMEN LIKE THEIR LIVES.

KATHARINE GRAHAM

"Together Forever"

**FEMINISM IS AN ENTIRE WORLD VIEW,
NOT JUST A LAUNDRY LIST OF 'WOMEN'S ISSUES'.**
CHARLOTTE BUNCH

When they told me that by the year 2100
women would rule the world,
my reply was, 'Still?'
WINSTON CHURCHILL

Genuine equality between
the sexes can only be realised in the
process of the socialist transformation
of society as a whole.
MAO TSE-TUNG

**YOU DON'T KNOW A WOMAN UNTIL
YOU HAVE HAD A LETTER FROM HER.**
ADA LEVERSON

"FAMILY"

If you want anything said, ask a man.
If you want something done, ask a woman.
MARGARET THATCHER

*Instead of this absurd division into sexes, they
ought to class people as static and dynamic.*
EVELYN WAUGH

Women who seek to be equal with men lack ambition.

TIMOTHY LEARY

THERE IS, HIDDEN OR FLAUNTED,
A SWORD BETWEEN THE SEXES TILL AN
ENTIRE MARRIAGE RECONCILES THEM.
C.S. LEWIS

"Together Forever".

Whatever women do they must do twice as well as men to be thought half as good. Luckily this is not difficult.

CHARLOTTE WHITTON

WOMEN ARE NEVER DISARMED BY COMPLIMENTS. MEN ALWAYS ARE. THAT IS THE DIFFERENCE BETWEEN THE SEXES.

OSCAR WILDE

A man never knows how to say goodbye; a woman never knows when to say it.

HELEN ROWLAND

The thing women have yet to learn is nobody gives you power. You just take it.

ROSEANNE BARR

"FAMILY"

I have a brain and a uterus,
and I use them both.

PATRICIA SCHROEDER

The only thing experience teaches us
is that experience teaches us nothing.

ANDRÉ MAUROIS

Women priests. Great, great. Now there's
priests of both sexes I don't listen to.

BILL HICKS

Age is a question of mind over matter.
If you don't mind, it doesn't matter.

SATCHEL PAIGE

"Together Forever"

I have a problem about being nearly 60:
I keep waking up in the morning
and thinking I'm 31.

ELIZABETH JANEWAY

Women marry men hoping they will change.

Men marry women hoping they will not.

So each is inevitably disappointed.

ALBERT EINSTEIN

True maturity is only reached when a
man realises he has become a father
figure to his girlfriends' boyfriends –
and he accepts it.

LARRY MCMURTRY

Man was made at the end
of the week's work,
when God was tired.

MARK TWAIN

"FAMILY"

Experience is a good teacher,
but she sends in terrific bills.

MINNA ANTRIM

OPPORTUNITY KNOCKS FOR EVERY MAN,
BUT YOU HAVE TO GIVE A WOMAN A RING.

MAE WEST

MY BEST BIRTH CONTROL NOW IS
JUST TO LEAVE THE LIGHTS ON.

JOAN RIVERS

A MAN'S FACE IS HIS AUTOBIOGRAPHY.
A WOMAN'S FACE IS HER WORK OF FICTION.

OSCAR WILDE

"Together Forever"

Age is not important unless you're a cheese.

HELEN HAYES

*I think that men are afraid
to be with a successful woman,
because we are terribly strong,
we know what we want and
we are not fragile enough.*

SHIRLEY BASSEY

Human beings, who are almost unique
in having the ability to learn from the
experience of others, are also remarkable
for their apparent disinclination to do so.

DOUGLAS ADAMS

*THERE'S SOMETHING LUXURIOUS
ABOUT HAVING A GIRL LIGHT YOUR
CIGARETTE. IN FACT, I GOT MARRIED
ONCE ON ACCOUNT OF THAT.*

HAROLD ROBBINS

"FAMILY"

CHERISH ALL YOUR HAPPY MOMENTS:
THEY MAKE A FINE CUSHION FOR OLD AGE.
CHRISTOPHER MORLEY

After you've done a thing the same way
for two years, look it over carefully.
After five years look at it with suspicion
... and after ten throw it away and start all over again.
ALFRED PERLMAN

The joy that isn't shared dies young.
ANNE SEXTON

I have an idea that the phrase 'weaker sex'
was coined by some woman to disarm some
man she was preparing to overwhelm.
OGDEN NASH

"Together Forever"

I don't think everyone has the right to happiness or to be loved.
Even the Americans have written into their constitution that
you have the right to the 'pursuit of happiness'.
You have the right to try – but that is all.

CLAIRE RAYNER

*IT IS ONLY WITH THE HEART
THAT ONE CAN SEE RIGHTLY;
WHAT IS ESSENTIAL IS
INVISIBLE TO THE EYE.*

ANTOINE DE SAINT-EXUPÉRY

A highbrow is a man who has found something
more interesting than women.

EDGAR WALLACE

I am a fatalist and believe
that what will be, will; what is, is;
and what was, was; and so on through the verbs.

LENNIE LOWER

"FAMILY"

*If women didn't exist,
all the money in the world
would have no meaning.*
ARISTOTLE ONASSIS

**May my husband rest in peace
till I get there.**
DAME EDNA EVERAGE

*A WOMAN SHOULD SOFTEN
BUT NOT WEAKEN A MAN.*
SIGMUND FREUD

" FRIENDS "

God's apology
for relations.

HUGH
KINGSMILL

"Best of Friends"

I do not believe that friends are necessarily the people you like best, they are merely the people who got there first.

PETER USTINOV

Thus nature has no love for solitude, and always leans, as it were, on some support; and the sweetest support is found in the most intimate friendship.

CICERO

A friend may well be reckoned the masterpiece of Nature.

RALPH WALDO EMERSON

"Best of Friends"

A FRIEND IS A SECOND SELF.
ARISTOTLE

THE FEELING OF FRIENDSHIP IS LIKE THAT
OF BEING COMFORTABLY FILLED WITH ROAST BEEF;
LOVE, LIKE BEING ENLIVENED WITH CHAMPAGNE.
JAMES BOSWELL

Friends help you move.
Real friends help you move bodies.
MILTON BERLE

IT IS ONE OF THE BLESSINGS OF OLD FRIENDS THAT
YOU CAN AFFORD TO BE STUPID WITH THEM.
RALPH WALDO EMERSON

"FRIENDS"

**I will speak ill of no man,
and speak all the good
I know of everybody.**
BENJAMIN FRANKLIN

The great thing about befriending
recovering alcoholics is that
you're never short of a ride home.
BILLY CONNOLLY

Treat your friends
as you do your pictures,
and place them in their best light.
JENNIE JEROME CHURCHILL

CHAMPAGNE FOR MY REAL FRIENDS;
REAL PAIN FOR MY SHAM FRIENDS.
FRANCIS BACON

"Best of Friends"

**DO NOT REMOVE A FLY FROM YOUR
FRIEND'S FOREHEAD WITH A HATCHET.**

CHINESE PROVERB

My mother used to say,
'There are no strangers,
only friends you haven't met yet.'
She's now in a maximum
security twilight home in Australia.

DAME EDNA EVERAGE

YOUR FRIEND IS THE MAN WHO KNOWS
ALL ABOUT YOU AND STILL LIKES YOU.

ELBERT HUBBARD

THE LION AND THE CALF
SHOULD LIE DOWN TOGETHER,
BUT THE CALF WON'T GET MUCH SLEEP.

WOODY ALLEN

"FRIENDS"

**Be slow to fall into friendship,
but when you are in, continue firm and constant.**
SOCRATES

There is no spectacle more agreeable than
to observe an old friend fall from a rooftop.
CONFUCIUS

Whenever a friend succeeds,
a little something in me dies.
GORE VIDAL

I prefer acquaintances to friends.
They don't expect you to call or
go to their children's weddings.
A.A. GILL

"Best of Friends"

FRIENDSHIP WITH ONESELF IS ALL-IMPORTANT BECAUSE WITHOUT IT ONE CANNOT BE FRIENDS WITH ANYONE ELSE IN THE WORLD.
ELEANOR ROOSEVELT

A true friend unbosoms freely, advises justly, assists readily, adventures boldly, defends courageously and continues a friend unchangeably.
WILLIAM PENN

If we were all given by magic the power to read each other's thoughts, I suppose the first effect would be to dissolve all friendships.
BERTRAND RUSSELL

"FRIENDS"

If a man does not make new acquaintance
as he advances through life, he will soon find himself left alone.
A man, sir, should keep his friendship in constant repair.

SAMUEL JOHNSON

My friends are my estate.

EMILY DICKINSON

Every man should keep a fair-sized cemetery
in which to bury the faults of his friends.

HENRY WARD BEECHER

**The better part of a man's life
consists of his friendships.**

ABRAHAM LINCOLN

"Best of Friends"

**NO MAN IS AN ISLAND, ENTIRE OF ITSELF.
EACH IS A PIECE OF THE CONTINENT,
A PART OF THE MAIN.**

JOHN DONNE

The greatest good you can do for another
is not just to share your riches,
but to reveal to him his own.

BENJAMIN DISRAELI

Maturity begins to grow when you
can sense your concern for others
outweighing your concern for yourself.

JOHN MacNAUGHTON

**NEVER KEEP UP WITH THE JONESES.
DRAG THEM DOWN TO YOUR LEVEL.**

QUENTIN CRISP

"FRIENDS"

There are two types of people – those who come into a room and say 'Well, here I am!' and those who come in and say 'Ah, there you are.'.
FREDERICK L. COLLINS

Those friends thou hast, and their adoption tried,

Grapple them to thy soul with hoops of steel;

But do not dull thy palm with entertainment

Of each new-hatch'd, unfledg'd comrade.
WILLIAM SHAKESPEARE

Each has his past shut in him like the leaves of a book known to him by heart and his friends can only read the title.
VIRGINIA WOOLF

"Best of Friends"

**IN THE END, WE WILL REMEMBER
NOT THE WORDS OF OUR ENEMIES,
BUT THE SILENCE OF OUR FRIENDS.**
MARTIN LUTHER KING

I can trust my friends.
These people force me to examine,
encourage me to grow.
CHER

I don't want to express an opinion.
You see, I have friends in both places.
MARK TWAIN (ON HEAVEN AND HELL)

TREAT PEOPLE AS IF THEY ARE WHAT THEY
OUGHT TO BE AND YOU HELP THEM TO BECOME
WHAT THEY ARE CAPABLE OF BEING.
GOETHE

The next best thing to being wise oneself is to live in a circle of those who are.

C.S. LEWIS

The main things which seem to me important on their own account, and not merely as means to other things, are knowledge, art, instinctive happiness, and relations of friendship or affection.

BERTRAND RUSSELL

LISTENING IS A MAGNETIC AND STRANGE THING, A CREATIVE FORCE. THE FRIENDS WHO LISTEN TO US ARE THE ONES WE MOVE TOWARD. WHEN WE ARE LISTENED TO, IT CREATES US, MAKES US UNFOLD AND EXPAND.

KARL MENNINGER

Good friends, good books and a sleepy conscience: this is the ideal life.

MARK TWAIN

"Best of Friends"

I HOLD THIS TO BE THE HIGHEST TASK FOR A BOND BETWEEN TWO PEOPLE: THAT EACH PROTECTS THE SOLITUDE OF THE OTHER.

RAINER MARIA RILKE

You cannot be lonely if
you like the person
you're alone with.

WAYNE DYER

I find friendship to be like wine,
raw when new, ripened with age,
the true old man's milk
and restorative cordial.

THOMAS JEFFERSON

AT A DINNER PARTY ONE SHOULD
EAT WISELY BUT NOT TOO WELL,
AND TALK WELL BUT NOT TOO WISELY.

W. SOMERSET MAUGHAM

"FRIENDS"

The lintel low enough to keep out pomp and pride;
The threshold high enough to turn deceit aside;
The doorband strong enough from robbers to defend;
This door will open at a touch to welcome every friend.

HENRY JACKSON VAN DYKE

*Wine is a treacherous friend
who you must always be on guard for.*

CHRISTIAN NESTELL BOVEE

Friends have all things in common.

PLATO

"Best of Friends"

EVERY TIME I PAINT A PORTRAIT I LOSE A FRIEND.

JOHN SINGER SARGENT

Anybody can sympathise
with the sufferings of a friend,
but it requires a very fine nature to
sympathise with a friend's success.

OSCAR WILDE

Without friends no one would choose to live,
though he had all other goods.

ARISTOTLE

"FRIENDS"

TEARS SHED FOR SELF ARE TEARS OF WEAKNESS, BUT TEARS SHED FOR OTHERS ARE A SIGN OF STRENGTH.
BILLY GRAHAM

No soul is desolate as long as there is a human being for whom it can feel trust and reverence.
GEORGE ELIOT

You must give some time to your fellow men. Even if it's a little thing, do something for others – something for which you get no pay but the privilege of doing it.
ALBERT SCHWEITZER

IT IS A SWEET THING, FRIENDSHIP, A DEAR BALM, A HAPPY AND AUSPICIOUS BIRD OF CALM.
PERCY BYSSHE SHELLEY

"Best of Friends"

**We cannot hold a torch to light another's path
without brightening our own.**
BEN SWEETLAND

I, no doubt, deserved my enemies,
but I don't believe I deserved my friends.
WALT WHITMAN

The service we render to others
is really the rent we pay for
our room on this earth.
WILFRED GRENFELL

FRIENDS ARE BORN, NOT MADE.
HENRY ADAMS

"FRIENDS"

What we have done for ourselves alone dies with us; what we have done for others and the world remains and is immortal.

ALBERT PIKE

This communicating of a man's self to his friend works
two contrary effects; for it redoubleth joy,
and cutteth griefs in half.

FRANCIS BACON

Misfortune shows those
who are not really friends.

ARISTOTLE

My best friend ran away with my wife
and, let me tell you, I miss him.

HENRY YOUNGMAN

Never look down on anybody
unless you're helping him up.

JESSE JACKSON

It is always painful to part from people
whom one has known for a very brief
space of time. The absence of old friends
one can endure with equanimity.

OSCAR WILDE

**A DAY WASTED ON OTHERS IS
NOT WASTED ON ONE'S SELF.**

CHARLES DICKENS

Friends were like clothes:
fine while they lasted but eventually
they wore thin or you grew out of them.

DAVID NICHOLLS

"FRIENDS"

**Friendship is certainly the finest balm
for the pangs of disappointed love.**

JANE AUSTEN

Often we have no time for our
friends but all the time in the
world for our enemies.

LEON URIS

It's the friends you can call up
at 4am that matter.

MARLENE DIETRICH

Outside of a dog, a book is man's best friend.
Inside of a dog it's too dark to read.

GROUCHO MARX

" Best of Friends "

**THE BEST WAY TO CHEER YOURSELF UP
IS TO TRY TO CHEER SOMEBODY ELSE UP.**

MARK TWAIN

We are here on earth to do good to others.
What the others are here for, I don't know.

W.H. AUDEN

When people talk, listen completely.
Most people never listen.

ERNEST HEMINGWAY

I GET BY WITH A LITTLE HELP FROM MY FRIENDS.

JOHN LENNON

"FRIENDS"

Do not be awestruck by other people and try to copy them. Nobody can be you as efficiently as you can.

NORMAN VINCENT PEALE

True friends stab you in the front.

OSCAR WILDE

The bird a nest, the spider a web, man friendship.

WILLIAM BLAKE

If you judge people, you have no time to love them.

MOTHER TERESA

YOU CANNOT SHAKE HANDS WITH A CLENCHED FIST.

INDIRA GANDHI

Grief can take care of itself,
but to get the full value of joy
you must have somebody
to divide it with.

MARK TWAIN

Friendship needs no words.
It is solitude delivered from
the anguish of loneliness.

DAG HAMMARSKJÖLD

THERE IS MAGIC IN THE MEMORY OF SCHOOLBOY
FRIENDSHIPS; IT SOFTENS THE HEART,
AND EVEN AFFECTS THE NERVOUS SYSTEM
OF THOSE WHO HAVE NO HEART.

BENJAMIN DISRAELI

"Best of Enemies"

Forgive your enemies,
but never forget their names.
JOHN F. KENNEDY

Abatement in the hostility
of one's enemies must never
be thought to signify that
they have been won over.
It only means that one has
ceased to constitute a threat.
QUENTIN CRISP

You can discover what your enemy
fears most by observing the means
he uses to frighten you.
ERIC HOFFER

" Best of Enemies "

It is easier to forgive an enemy
than to forgive a friend.

WILLIAM BLAKE

DEAN MARTIN COULD MAKE A PLATE
OF COOKED SPAGHETTI SEEM TENSE.

FRANK SINATRA

You must not fight too often with one enemy,
or you will teach him all your art of war.

NAPOLEON BONAPARTE

Few things are harder to put up
with than the annoyance
of a good example.

MARK TWAIN

this is page
149

"FRIENDS"

**I hate admitting that
my enemies have a point.**

SALMAN RUSHDIE

Vulgarity is simply
the conduct of other people.

OSCAR WILDE

A man may learn wisdom
even from a foe.

ARISTOPHANES

You shall judge of a man by his
foes as well as by his friends.

JOSEPH CONRAD

" Best of Enemies "

THE BEST WEAPON AGAINST AN ENEMY IS ANOTHER ENEMY.

FRIEDRICH NIETZSCHE

People wish their enemies dead, but I do not.
I say give them the gout, give them the stone.

LADY MARY WORTLEY MONTAGU

He was a cock who thought the sun
had come up to hear him crow.

GEORGE ELIOT

I CHOOSE MY FRIENDS FOR THEIR GOOD LOOKS,
MY ACQUAINTANCES FOR THEIR GOOD CHARACTERS
AND MY ENEMIES FOR THEIR INTELLECTS.
A MAN CANNOT BE TOO CAREFUL
IN THE CHOICE OF HIS ENEMIES.

OSCAR WILDE

**My sister, Jackie, is younger than me.
We don't know quite by how much.**
JOAN COLLINS

We often give our enemies
the means of our own destruction.
AESOP

*She's always nice to her inferiors,
whenever she can find them.*
DOROTHY PARKER

Let my enemies devour each other.
SALVADOR DALÍ

you're on page
152

IT IS HARD TO FIGHT AN ENEMY WHO HAS OUTPOSTS IN YOUR HEAD.

SALLY KEMPTON

I went to Switzerland and got an obscene yodel.

RODNEY DANGERFIELD

For a person who cherishes compassion and love, the practice of tolerance is essential; and, for that, an enemy is indispensable.

DALAI LAMA

SHE HAS AN EGO LIKE A RAGING TOOTH.

W.B. YEATS

"FRIENDS"

You have many enemies that know not why they are so,
but, like to village curs, bark when their fellows do.
WILLIAM SHAKESPEARE

I don't hold with abroad and
think that foreigners speak English
when our backs are turned.
QUENTIN CRISP

Enemies are so stimulating.
KATHARINE HEPBURN

Winston Churchill would make a drum
out of the skin of his own mother,
the louder to sing his own praises.
DAVID LLOYD GEORGE

YE HAVE HEARD THAT IT HATH BEEN SAID,
THOU SHALT LOVE THY NEIGHBOUR,
AND HATE THINE ENEMY. BUT I SAY UNTO YOU,
LOVE YOUR ENEMIES, BLESS THEM THAT CURSE YOU,
DO GOOD TO THEM THAT HATE YOU,
AND PRAY FOR THEM WHICH DESPITEFULLY USE
YOU, AND PERSECUTE YOU...

THE BIBLE (GOSPEL OF MATTHEW)

I don't like Norwegians at all.
The sun never sets, the bar never opens
and the whole country smells of kippers.

EVELYN WAUGH

Beware the wrath
of a patient adversary.

JOHN C. CALHOUN

DON'T BE SO HUMBLE.
YOU'RE NOT THAT GREAT.

GOLDA MEIR

"FRIENDS"

**Money can't buy friends,
but it can get you a better class of enemy.**
SPIKE MILLIGAN

A Scotsman is a man who,
before sending his pyjamas to the laundry,
stuffs a sock in each pocket.
AMBROSE BIERCE

When my enemies stop hissing,
I shall know I'm slipping.
MARIA CALLAS

Start off every day with a smile
and get it over with.
W.C. FIELDS

" Best of Enemies "

O LORD, MAKE MY ENEMIES RIDICULOUS.

VOLTAIRE

The Irish is one race of people for whom
psychoanalysis is of no use whatsoever.

SIGMUND FREUD

A wise man gets more use from
his enemies than a fool from his friends.

BALTASAR GRACIAN

IT WAS A DELIGHTFUL VISIT;
PERFECT IN BEING MUCH TOO SHORT.

JANE AUSTEN

"FRIENDS"

After all, what is your host's purpose in having a party?
Surely not for you to enjoy yourself; if that
were their sole purpose, they'd have simply sent
champagne and women over to your place by taxi.
P.J. O'ROURKE

Going to war without France
is like going deer hunting
without an accordion.
GENERAL NORMAN SCHWARZKOPF

Hospitality consists in a little fire,
a little food, and an immense quiet.
RALPH WALDO EMERSON

I told my mother-in-law that my
house was her house and she said,
'Get the hell off my property.'
JOAN RIVERS

" *Best of Enemies* "

YOU MUST COME AGAIN WHEN YOU HAVE LESS TIME.
WALTER SICKERT

Belgium is a country invented by
the British to annoy the French.
CHARLES DE GAULLE

Fish and visitors stink
after three days.
BENJAMIN FRANKLIN

The British film industry is just
a bunch of people in London
who can't get green cards.
ALAN PARKER

"FRIENDS"

Some cause happiness wherever they go;
others whenever they go.

OSCAR WILDE

*If you can't say anything
good about someone,
sit right here by me.*

ALICE ROOSEVELT LONGWORT

So you're from Windsor.
They have some lovely homes there.
Do you live near any of them?

DAME EDNA EVERAGE

*John Prescott has the face of a man
who clubs baby seals to death.*

DENIS HEALEY

" Best of Enemies "

**DINNER PARTIES ARE GIVEN MOSTLY
IN THE MIDDLE CLASSES BY WAY OF REVENGE.**

WILLIAM MAKEPIECE THACKERAY

Television has proved that people will look
at anything rather than each other.

ANN LANDERS

When everyone is against you,
it means that you are absolutely
wrong or absolutely right.

ALBERT GUINON

**OF COURSE, AMERICA HAD OFTEN BEEN
DISCOVERED BEFORE COLUMBUS, BUT
IT HAD ALWAYS BEEN HUSHED UP.**

OSCAR WILDE

"FRIENDS"

There's nothing more boring than
a really beautiful person
who has nothing to say.
GWYNETH PALTROW

A crust eaten in peace is better than
a banquet partaken in anxiety.
AESOP

There is nothing in the world more reassuring
than an unhappy lottery winner.
TONY PARSONS

Santa Claus has the right idea;
visit people once a year.
VICTOR BORGE

" Best of Enemies "

NO MATTER HOW MANY CHAIRS YOU PROVIDE, GUESTS ALWAYS SIT ON THE EDGE OF A LITTLE TABLE AND KNOCK SHERRY ON THE CARPET.
PAUL JENNINGS

War doesn't determine who's right . . . only who's left.
BERTRAND RUSSELL

In England people actually try to be brilliant at breakfast. That is so dreadful of them! Only dull people are brilliant at breakfast.
OSCAR WILDE

I'VE NEVER STRUCK A WOMAN IN MY LIFE . . . NOT EVEN MY OWN MOTHER.
W.C. FIELDS

"FRIENDS"

An alcoholic is a man you don't like who drinks as much as you do.

DYLAN THOMAS

Clement Atlee is a modest little man with much to be modest about.

WINSTON CHURCHILL

At every party there are two kinds of people – those who want to go home and those who don't. The trouble is, they are usually married to each other.

ANN LANDERS

Life is difficult enough without Meryl Streep movies.

TRUMAN CAPOTE

" Best of Enemies "

THE TELEPHONE IS A GOOD WAY TO TALK TO PEOPLE
WITHOUT HAVING TO OFFER THEM A DRINK.
FRAN LEBOWITZ

Never give a party if you will be
the most interesting person there.
MICKEY FRIEDMAN

*You always knew exactly where you were
with Errol Flynn because he
always let you down.*
DAVID NIVEN

ESTATE AGENTS ARE JUST PEOPLE WHO DIDN'T
MAKE IT AS SECOND-HAND CAR SALESMEN.
BILLY CONNOLLY

"FRIENDS"

The hardest thing in life is to know which bridge to cross and which to burn.

DAVID RUSSELL

It is a man's own mind, not his enemy or foe, that lures him to evil ways.

BUDDHA

He has all the virtues I dislike and none of the vices I admire.

WINSTON CHURCHILL

A friend is one who has the same enemies as you have.

ABRAHAM LINCOLN

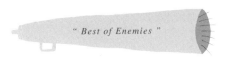
" Best of Enemies "

**HIS LACK OF EDUCATION IS
MORE THAN COMPENSATED FOR
BY HIS KEENLY DEVELOPED MORAL BANKRUPTCY.**
WOODY ALLEN

I have met the enemy,
and it is the eyes of other people.
BENJAMIN FRANKLIN

One of the good things about getting
older is you find you're more interesting
than most of the people you meet.
LEE MARVIN

**NEVER INTERRUPT YOUR ENEMY
WHEN HE IS MAKING A MISTAKE.**
NAPOLEON BONAPARTE

"FRIENDS"

Some people can stay longer in an hour than others can in a week.

WILLIAM DEAN HOWELLS

A doubtful friend is worse than a certain enemy.

AESOP

Her virtue was that she said what she thought, her vice that what she thought didn't amount to much.

PETER USTINOV

Whenever, at a party, I have been in the mood to study fools, I have always looked for a great beauty: they always gather round her like flies around a fruit stall.

JEAN PAUL RICHTER

" *Best of Enemies* "

**I DIDN'T ATTEND THE FUNERAL, BUT I SENT A NICE
LETTER SAYING THAT I APPROVED OF IT.**
MARK TWAIN

Like other parties of the kind, it was first silent,
then talky, then argumentative, then disputatious,
then unintelligible, then altogethery,
then inarticulate, and then drunk.
LORD BYRON

I don't like country music,
but I don't mean to denigrate those who do.
And for the people who like country music,
denigrate means put down.
BOB NEWHART

**YOU HAVE ENEMIES? GOOD. THAT MEANS YOU'VE
STOOD UP FOR SOMETHING SOMETIME IN YOUR LIFE.**
WINSTON CHURCHILL

this is page
169

"FRIENDS"

**Sometimes when you look in his eyes
you get the feeling that someone else is driving.**
DAVID LETTERMAN

We have real enemies in the world.
These enemies must be found.
They must be pursued and
they must be defeated.
BARACK OBAMA

It is equally offensive to speed a guest who would like to stay
and to detain one who is anxious to leave.
HOMER

*I have never made but one prayer to God,
a very short one – 'Oh, Lord, make my
enemies ridiculous.' And God granted it.*
VOLTAIRE

" Best of Enemies "

**A BANQUET IS PROBABLY THE MOST FATIGUING
THING IN THE WORLD – EXCEPT DITCHDIGGING.**
MARK TWAIN

I ask you to judge me
by the enemies I have made.
FRANKLIN D. ROOSEVELT

*What's on your mind,
if you will allow the overstatement?*
FRED ALLEN

LOVERS MAY BE – AND INDEED GENERALLY ARE
– ENEMIES, BUT THEY NEVER CAN BE FRIENDS,
BECAUSE THERE MUST ALWAYS BE A SPICE OF
JEALOUSY AND A SOMETHING OF SELF
IN ALL THEIR SPECULATIONS.
LORD BYRON

"FRIENDS"

He is one of those people who would be enormously improved by death.

SAKI

Only enemies speak the truth – friends and lovers lie endlessly, caught in the web of duty.

STEPHEN KING

The Life and Soul, the man who will never go home while there is one man, woman or glass of anything not yet drunk.

KATHARINE WHITEHORN

IT TAKES A GREAT DEAL OF BRAVERY TO STAND UP TO OUR ENEMIES, BUT JUST AS MUCH TO STAND UP TO OUR FRIENDS.

J.K. ROWLING

He has all the characteristics of a dog
– except loyalty.

SAM HOUSTON

FINE WORDS!
I WONDER WHERE YOU STOLE THEM.

JONATHAN SWIFT

**His shortcoming is
his long staying.**

BENJAMIN DISRAELI

*At the end of every party
there is always a girl crying.*

PETER KAY

No one can have a
higher opinion of him than I have,
and I think he's a dirty little beast.

W.S. GILBERT

A waste of skin.

LANCASHIRE EXPRESSION

You have delighted us long enough.

JANE AUSTEN

**Gossip is when you hear something
you like about someone you don't.**

EARL WILSON

For three days after death, hair and fingernails continue to grow but phone calls taper off.
JOHNNY CARSON

He can compress the most words into the smallest ideas of any man I ever met.
ABRAHAM LINCOLN

I never forget a face, but in your case I'll be glad to make an exception.
GROUCHO MARX

I heard his library burned down and both books were destroyed – and one of them hadn't even been coloured in yet.
ROBERTSON DAVIES

*Is it not the sweetest mockery
to mock our enemies?*

SOPHOCLES

I'm just grateful to be on this planet.
I have no enemies that I know of.
I'm just the guy who makes [people] happy.

CHUBBY CHECKER

AM I NOT DESTROYING MY ENEMIES
WHEN I MAKE FRIENDS OF THEM?

ABRAHAM LINCOLN

If you don't have enemies,
you don't have character.

PAUL NEWMAN